## ENDORSEMENTS

*Reading* Soul's Journey *is feeling the blood rushing in your veins, smelling the fragrance of the consciousness, tasting the reality of your emotions, listening to the melody of the universe, embracing vulnerability.*

*Soul's Journey is a journey on its own. The magic of Sam Yau is shaped by his profound humanity, his moving story, from the baby he was to the father he is, with his many facets of man's essence…*

*If Expression was to be but a recipe, Soul's Journey is an extraordinary composition: a delicate dance between insightful words and wonderful illustrations. This collection is an invitation to let poetry infuse you with its mysterious art.*

Sophie Roumeas<br>
Mindful Therapies (Meditation, Hypnosis, Systemic Constellation)<br>
Training Auravision™

*Few poems have moved me as deeply as these. The author's voice seems to capture the perfect union of spirit, nature, the human condition, and the infinite search for truth and beauty that transcends religion or philosophy. The transformative beauty of these words appeals to me more as a daily meditation—something to ground me in consciousness and inspire me to practice their wisdom in my own life. Sam Yau is truly a sage for our times and a poet whose meaning and purpose can shed light on the many challenges we face within and without.*

Raoul Goff<br>
Publisher & CEO, Mandala Publishing

*Sam Yau in his infinite beautiful creative and truthful vision of soul eternal life in his new book* Soul's Journey *has moved my saddened heart and validates with his poetry and Olena Zavakevych's artwork what lives within me: an uncompromising spirit of unconditional love for nature man and spirit. This week I sadly buried my younger sister and God in his infinite wisdom sent me this powerful book of love in poetic form to brighten my day and remember my sister lives beyond this physical world. She was a poet and artist also. Sam wrote, "May I cross the bridge between realms. I am a soul. I was never born. I will never die. Love will never end. May I live with awareness of veiled truths while shrouded in human form." This book shares a message of awareness of the depth of our being that all readers may benefit from.*

Sheryl Glick
Host of Internet Radio Show "Healing from Within"
Energy Soul Healer/Medium
www.sherylglick.com

*The first time I heard Sam Yau's poetry I wanted to cry. It pierces the layers of illusion, but with a gentleness that soothes rather than condemns. 'You are a soul incarnated in the human school to learn to love,' he spoke. How many times had I spoken those very words looking into the questioning eyes of my hospice patients of all faiths, cultures and persuasions…*

*Sam's poetry is universal, and yet it has distinct wisdom echoes of the Upanishads and Bhagavad Gita, the Dao De Ching and the I Ching, the New Testament and the Dhammapada, quantum physics and cosmology. A renaissance man who calls out from the depths of brokenness and lived experience, reaching a hand to each of us as a brother or sister on the path home.*

*Sam guides us to see the beautiful strengths and uniqueness of each living being woven within the certitude of an unbreakable oneness with the All That Is. His is a still small voice from a man of great power and humility. It is not hard to hear if we listen carefully—to his poetry, and to the inner and outer worlds that we inhabit. His message gently reminds us of the optimistic and great journey here, now, and unfolding before us.*

Phillip Jones, Psychotherapist<br>
Author of *Transcendence: Finding Peace at the End of Life*

*The Soul's Journey* is a wonderful breath of fresh air at a pivotal time in our world history. Sam Yau's book of poetry shines the light of hope during this time of extreme duress, providing soothing solace to those who are open to elevated conscious awareness. His gently inspiring words flow easily into our hearts, as they touch our minds and spirits with the grace of peace. This lovely book is also beautiful in its aesthetic design with softly inspiring imagery throughout by the gifted artist, Olena Zavakevych. I anticipate having a copy of this tenderly compelling book on my coffee table for daily inspiration and ongoing encouragement. Thank you, Sam, for sharing this heartfelt treasure.

Lois Hermann, Author, Spiritual Mentor, Catalyst for Positive Change
Award-Winning Author of #1 Best Seller *Chronicles of Hope,* and *Spirits of Amoskeag*
www.LoisHermann.com / www.ChroniclesofHope.net

I have always known Sam Yau as a traveling soul with a deep-felt higher consciousness and a seeker of Truth. Sam's poetry is a mystical manifestation of his own soul journey, and therefore my own and all souls at some collective level. He has an amazing ability to transcribe an answer to our question of, "Why am I Here? Am I a cosmic accident, or am I here for some purpose?" Sam has reinforced the absolute answer that we are here for a soul-purpose. My oneness with Sam, others, and the universe is to live this life as a spiritual being in a human existence—to experience pleasure and pain, forgiveness and love with all of our felt-emotions injected into the growth of our soul. This poetic expression accelerates this process, wrapped in exquisite self-discovery. What a beautiful round-trip expressed so eloquently yet simply by Sam—from the inception of our being to a return to our spiritual home with a higher level of consciousness in and for our collective One. Thank you, Sam.

Tom Zender
CEO Mentor and Leadership Developer
Former President & CEO of Unity

*Soul's Journey is the love of a father painted in words for his son, transcending time, space, and this world. I felt utterly captivated by the ebb and flow of the words and connected to the very essence of a being. This book of poetry will take you on a journey to realize what truly matters and why it is important to cherish what matters. Let your soul be moved. Take the walk with Sam Yau and let your spirit feel; feel the pure beauty and pain of love to embrace it wholeheartedly.*

Dr. Kasthuri Henry, PhD
Founder of Ennobled For Success Institute
#1 International Best-Selling Author
www.kashenry.com

*Sam Yau's beautiful book of poetry deeply explores his life and the human condition. As you read you feel love, deep grief and the mystic connections from quantum physics made personal. He looks inside himself to find his soul's journey and lifts you into your own exploration. As a poet I am impressed and inspired. This is an important work of art.*

Paul David Walker
Poet, Philosopher, and Advisor to Leaders
CEO & Founder, Genius Stone Partners

*This glorious collection of poetry and images will quench the hungry heart of anyone who has lost a loved one or pondered life on the other side. Taking you on a sometimes-painful expedition into consciousness these poems serve as a guide into the peace and unity of love and the eternalness of the soul. Thank you, Sam, for this beautiful healing collection of poems.*

Aeriol Ascher, MsD
Founder of the Healing Body Mind and Soul Network

*The poetry of Sam Yau comes from a place of 'other', a place of the Sacred. Sam touches us at the depths of our humanity and soul, each and every word a message from the Divine. Sam's poetry is a unique gift to the world that transforms, inspires, and transmutes us all.*

Dr. Lisa L. Rayburn, Esq.
CEO of The Détente Foundation

*Sam Yau's poetry ignited a profound healing activation within my heart. As I read his poems, they activated a new compassion for the pain I still had buried within it. I understood what unconditional love meant. There should never be any conditions to love no matter the pain and hurt we carry. Through our heart we can see and love without judgement, without exceptions and without limits. With gratitude and love, thank you, Sam, for opening your heart and putting your love into these pages.*

Renee Vidal
Akashic Records Quantum Healer

*In Soul's Journey, Sam Yau takes you on an inner journey of traumatic loss and grief and gives you a peek into his process of healing and awakening. With boldness, courage, and sincerity, he paints the picture of the human condition with compassion and understanding while unflappably trusting the eternal—and reminding you of the power of love.*

Rúna Bouius
Founder, True Power Institute

*The Soul's Journey is the most powerful, enlightening, and healing book of poetry I have ever had the pleasure of laying my eyes and my soul upon. His poems are not just words. They feel as pure divine love that invokes this remembrance from within you. No matter if you're going through grief, trauma, feeling lost in life or walking a spiritual path; the wisdom and love within these pages connect you to pure inspiration to keep you moving forward. Everyone should read this book, you will laugh, cry, and remember your heart deeply.*

Kara Goss
Energy and Spiritual Healer

*Inspiring, comforting, and penetratingly honest—these are the words that come to me after reading Sam Yau's stunningly beautiful book of poetry. It is a living testament to the healing power of loving kindness, and a beckoning to all lightworkers to "wake humanity to its destiny of heaven on earth." I highly recommend his book!*

Bonnie Joy Walker
Fellow Spiritual Traveler and Writer from the Heart

# SOUL'S journey

## SAM YAU

### ORIGINAL ART BY OLENA ZAVAKEVYCH

**Soul's Journey**
Sam Yau
Clear Source Books

Published by Clear Source Books, Laguna Beach, CA
Copyright ©2021 Sam Yau (Ching Yuen)
All rights reserved.

Project Management and Book Design: Davis Creative, DavisCreative.com

Artist: Olena Zavakevych, the artist who was inspired by the poems to create the paintings

Poetry Coach: Rachel Kann

Publisher's Cataloging-In-Publication Data
(Prepared by The Donohue Group, Inc.)

Names: Yau, Sam, author. | Zavakevych, Olena, artist.

Title: Soul's journey / Sam Yau ; original art by Olena Zavakevych.

Description: Laguna Beach, CA : Clear Source Books, [2021]

Identifiers: ISBN 9781736370001 (paperback) | ISBN 9781736370018 (hardback) | ISBN 9781736370025 (ebook)

Subjects: LCSH: Spiritual healing--Poetry. | Self-actualization (Psychology)--Poetry. | Soul--Poetry. | Life change events--Poetry. | Loss (Psychology)--Poetry. | BISAC: BODY, MIND & SPIRIT / General. | SELF-HELP / Personal Growth / General. | SELF-HELP / Spiritual.

Classification: LCC PS3625.A8 S68 2021 (print) | LCC PS3625.A8 (ebook) | DDC 811/.6--dc23

2021

ATTENTION CORPORATIONS, UNIVERSITIES, COLLEGES AND PROFESSIONAL ORGANIZATIONS: Quantity discounts are available on bulk purchases of this book for educational, gift purposes, or as premiums for increasing magazine subscriptions or renewals. Special books or book excerpts can also be created to fit specific needs. For information, please contact Sam Yau, Sam@SamYauPoetry.com

## DEDICATION

To my son Ryan who returned to spirit in 2016.
His passing catapulted me onto my poetry journey upon his wings.

## GRATITUDE

I am grateful to:

Sophie Roumeas, for being the first to inspire me to write poems
and the first to see me as a poet of the soul.

Rachel Kann, for being an amazing coach showing me the path to become a poet.

Olena Zavakevych, for being my partner in art,
for her deep resonance with the content of my poetry,
for her gorgeous paintings that take my breath away.

And to many others who have supported me in my poetry journey, including:

Renee Furbush and Jen Sanford,
My brother Ernest Yau,
My sister Cecilia Yau.

# TABLE OF CONTENTS

Preface . . . . . . . . . . . . . . . . . . . . . . . . 1

**Soul's Journey**
    Soul's Journey . . . . . . . . . . . . . . . . . . 4
    A Prayer . . . . . . . . . . . . . . . . . . . . . . 8
    A Prayer II . . . . . . . . . . . . . . . . . . . . 14
    Do Not Let Anyone Tell You to Live Someone Else's Life . . . . . . . . . . . . 18
    Unity in Diversity . . . . . . . . . . . . . . . 20
    Who Am I? . . . . . . . . . . . . . . . . . . . 24

**Inner Garden**
    Inner Garden . . . . . . . . . . . . . . . . . 32
    Meditation . . . . . . . . . . . . . . . . . . . 36
    Gratitude . . . . . . . . . . . . . . . . . . . . 40
    Come Home . . . . . . . . . . . . . . . . . . 42
    Devour . . . . . . . . . . . . . . . . . . . . . . 44

**A Thousand Small Cuts**
    A Thousand Small Cuts . . . . . . . . . . 50
    Grief . . . . . . . . . . . . . . . . . . . . . . . . 54
    Darkness . . . . . . . . . . . . . . . . . . . . . 58
    Split . . . . . . . . . . . . . . . . . . . . . . . . 62
    Tapestry . . . . . . . . . . . . . . . . . . . . . 66

**Transfigured**
    Transfigured . . . . . . . . . . . . . . . . . . 72
    Walk with Me, My Son . . . . . . . . . . 78
    Unblemished . . . . . . . . . . . . . . . . . . 82
    My Spirit Friends . . . . . . . . . . . . . . . 86

**Science and Consciousness**
    Science and Consciousness . . . . . . . . 90
    The Gravity of Love . . . . . . . . . . . . . 96
    Collide . . . . . . . . . . . . . . . . . . . . . 100
    My Body . . . . . . . . . . . . . . . . . . . 104

**See with The Eyes of Our Heart**
    See with The Eyes of Our Heart . . . . 108
    I Can't Wait to Meet You . . . . . . . . 114
    Infused . . . . . . . . . . . . . . . . . . . . . 118
    Wine Tasting . . . . . . . . . . . . . . . . . 120
    Shadow . . . . . . . . . . . . . . . . . . . . 124
    Reverberate . . . . . . . . . . . . . . . . . . 126
    Parting . . . . . . . . . . . . . . . . . . . . . 130

**Nature**
    Nature . . . . . . . . . . . . . . . . . . . . . 134
    The Effortless Way of Tao . . . . . . . . 138
    Swept Away by the Tiniest Vibrations . . 144
    Clouds . . . . . . . . . . . . . . . . . . . . . 148

**Duende**
    Duende . . . . . . . . . . . . . . . . . . . . 158
    Kathmandu 2003 . . . . . . . . . . . . . 162
    Ode to Lucille Clifton . . . . . . . . . . 168

**A Summons to Lightworkers**
    A Summons to Lightworkers . . . . . . 172

About the Poet . . . . . . . . . . . . . . . . . . 179
About the Artist . . . . . . . . . . . . . . . . . 181

# PREFACE

In 2016, my son Ryan killed himself with a bullet through his brain.

The moment I heard the news I knew my life was changed forever.

To grieve, I retreated into seclusion. All my interests at that time dropped away.

For more than 20 years, I had been on a journey of personal and spiritual growth. I always knew that I am a spirit. With Ryan's death, and my desire to be close to him, simply knowing that I am a soul was no longer enough.

One day, a question was stuck in my mind that would not go away. What if I live as a soul in the human clothes, rather than as a human who has a soul. That pondering set in motion a startling inversion of priority. Asking my soul that question with persistence and commitment catapulted me into a surprising journey that I could not have imagined just a few years ago.

I received clear messages from Ryan and uncanny sources to write poems. I had never written a serious poem in my life. But my soul's whisper was unceasing. With a series of synchronicities and chance encounters, new friends became the angels in my poetry journey. The calling was unmistakable. I surrendered.

My verses, together with the love from my friends and family, have healed me. My poetic musings clarified, distilled, deepened and ingrained the essence of past spiritual experiences onto my being. As I sculpted my poems, my poems were sculpturing me at the same time. Writing poetry has become a most joyous and uplifting spiritual practice for me.

The soul's journey is one that discovers the true nature of the Divine and each soul is love itself. Peeling off all layers of reality, only awareness and love remain.

My poems have healed and transformed me, by sharing them I hope they will heal and inspire others.

# SOUL'S journey

Soul's Journey
A Prayer
A Prayer II
Do Not Let Anyone Tell You to Live Someone Else's Life
Unity in Diversity
Who Am I?

  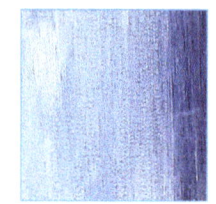   

# SOUL'S JOURNEY

# Soul's Journey

**Sam Yau**

The day you were born,
you were given four gifts:
self-awareness,
free will,
an ego,
and forgetfulness.

Who animates your heartbeat,
activates your breath,
comforts you when you are sad,
celebrates with you when you are joyful,
shines light through your darkest days,
surprises you with joy in your deepest sorrow?

Who awes you with
the sun's first beam that pierces the hilltop,
the sunset cloud that sprays golden rays,
the wind that waves the green wheat field,
the glint that bounces on a blanket of white snow?

Who nudges you to
seek meaning and purpose,
expand your circle of love,
arrive at the unity in diversity,
find your way back to Source?

You surge
from the ocean of awareness
as a desire of the Divine
to experience Itself as the unique you:
one strand of the infinite glory
and variety of Its creations.

You are a wave rising up to
the beautiful dance of life,
remerging into eternity.

Original painting by Olena Zavakevych
inspired by the poem, "Soul's Journey"

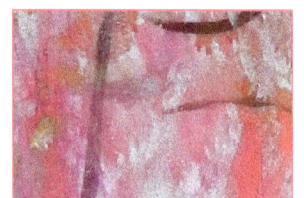     

# A PRAYER

# A Prayer

Love is the substance of the universe.
May I be a receptacle for it.
May it fill me to the brim
and overflow to anyone who comes upon my path.
May I be present with every sentient being
and bow to the divine spark shining in their soul.

May my heart expand to be more inclusive.
May my mind expand to be more loving
until I am one with the universe.

May I be present with my feelings
and my thoughts every moment of the day.
May I be aware of awareness itself,
and know that it is the nature of my being.
May I glimpse the fullest emptiness,
shimmering with all creative potentials.

May I become conscious of my habitual patterns,
catching them by the head and not the tail.
May I regain my freedom by not acting on them.
May I embrace and transcend my shadow,
choosing to dwell in my higher self.

# A Prayer

**Sam Yau**

May I empty and surrender this vessel
so that spirits may inspire and dance within me.
May I see what is unseen,
perceive what is not perceived,
remember what has been forgotten,
converse with my eternal truth,
walk amongst angels and guides,
with loved ones who have departed.
May I cross the bridge between realms.

I am a soul.
I was never born.
I will never die.
Love will never end.
May I live with the awareness
of these veiled truths
while shrouded in human form.

When the time comes for me to leave this life,
waking from this dream of my sojourn to earth,
I shall smile and celebrate my return home.

May we release our collective trauma.
May we all heal each other and be healed
by lovingkindness.

Original painting by Olena Zavakevych
inspired by the poem, "A Prayer"

  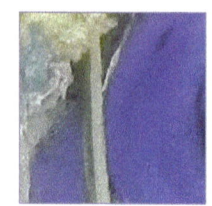   

# A
# PRAYER II

God is Love.
May I be present with others and
see God's image shining in their soul.

May light shine in my darkest days.
May I be filled with joy in my deepest sorrow.

God is in me.
I am in God.
May I be fully aware of these truths
while shrouded in human form.

May we love each other and be loved.
May we be the love God is.

Original painting by Olena Zavakevych
inspired by the poem, "A Prayer II"

# DO NOT LET ANYONE TELL YOU TO LIVE SOMEONE ELSE'S LIFE

## Do Not Let Anyone Tell You to Live Someone Else's Life

Do not let anyone tell you to live someone else's life.
You have a gift to co-create your special life with the divine.
Let the spark in you shine, live and dance like a unique spirit.

Shape your inner world with qualities that bring you delight.
Live inside out, the outside world will coalesce into your design.
Do not let anyone tell you to live someone else's life.

Listen to your inner voice from your soul and let it guide you, trust it.
Living the authentic you will bring you freedom and joy, claim it.
Let the spark in you shine, live and dance like a unique spirit.

You are a soul incarnated in the human school to learn to love,
You are frozen light that soon will take the soaring flight.
Do not let anyone tell you to live someone else's life.

Already connected to The Source, turn it on and drink it in.
Angels are always there to help if you let your intuition align.
Let the spark in you shine, live and dance like a unique spirit.

You have been knocking at the door from the inside all your life.
Turn around, you are perfect and totally lovable, live it.
Do not let anyone tell you to live someone else's life.
Let the spark in you shine, live and dance like a unique spirit.

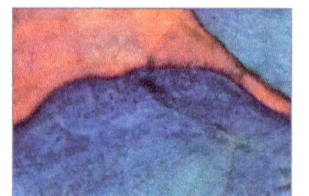

# UNITY IN DIVERSITY

# Unity in Diversity

*Sam Yau*

Fourteen billion years ago,
you and I were born
of stardust from
the explosive expansion
of the singularity.

We shared 99.9% of our genes,
co-evolved with all of life
in this rich biosphere of
amazing beauty and diversity.

Formless divinity preceded
the creation of form,
imbued it with —
and enveloped it in—
infinite love,

buried a spark in each of us,
a light to guide us to our source,

which is how the human mind
discovers the elegant simplicity
of mathematics that hold
the secrets of the universe,

which is how the human heart
knows we are deeply connected—
to all humanity,
to our divine origin,
to our collective imagination
and manifestation of our future—
in a glorious web.

Let's rejoice in
uniqueness,
the intimacy in sameness,
the admiration of difference.

Each of us,
a star shining in the tapestry
of galaxies in the celestial dome.

Original painting by Olena Zavakevych
inspired by the poem, "Unity in Diversity"

  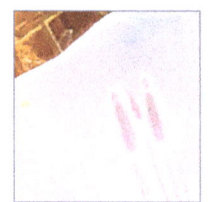   

# WHO AM I?

# Who Am I?

### Sam Yau

I see an oak tree.

What is the color of
its green leaves when
no one is there to see?

What is the sound
of a tree falling when
no one is there to hear?

My tears know
only my name.
I wonder if anyone will
ever know my pain?

Sometimes, a thought
drops into my mind
and I don't know
where it came from.

Senses,
feelings and
thoughts
are my only reality.

Who renders
experience from
sense and perception?

Who constructs
the self from
experience?

Who orchestrates
the symphony
of my life
with my brain?

I am that self-awareness,

from which there is a path
to cosmic consciousness.

The seeker,
the path,
neither are
different from
what is being sought.

# Who Am I?

**Sam Yau**

A pearl already has
all of nature in it.

A cell already has
all of life in it.

Who sets the precise
constants of nature that
fine-tune the cosmos
for life to emerge?

Consciousness
pervades all matter
in an unbroken whole.

The Many and the One
are the same.

I am aware, therefore I am.
I am awareness itself.

Photo by Sam Yau
for the poem, "Who Am I?"

# INNER *garden*

Inner Garden
Meditation
Gratitude
Come Home
Devour

# INNER GARDEN

# Inner Garden

**Sam Yau**

There was a time you worried
people would not be kind,
life would deal you a bad hand.

There is a garden inside of you.
You are its sole caretaker.
You can plant flowers of love.
You can sow seeds of wisdom.

When your garden is safe,
your world is safe.
When it is beautiful,
your world is beautiful.
When it is peaceful,
you become a peacemaker.

Your happiness comes from within,
no one can take it away from you.
When you are full inside, you see
the half-full in the world and fill it.
You see the best in others,
so they show their best to you.

People will be drawn to you,
events will coalesce into what you envision.

Your outer journey takes you
to the four corners of the earth.
Your inner one traverses
across the universe.

There is no outside world.
Every time you look outward,
it is a projection.

Tend your garden well.
Live inside-out.
The world you experience
is within you.

Original painting by Olena Zavakevych
inspired by the poem, "Inner Garden"

  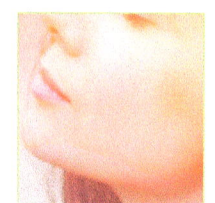  

# MEDITATION

# Meditation

*Sam Yau*

Thoughts fly into my mind's chamber
like uninvited birds.
Without attention from me,
they can no longer     latch
onto other thoughts.
New arrivals become spare.
One by one, they depart.

Without thoughts,
memories can't linger,
tomorrow can't emerge.
Without a flutter of past or future,
my feelings subside.

Lying still, I feel
each pulsation in my wrist,
the throbbing at my toes' tips.
I hear the thundering rumbling
and growling in my guts,
the whirling and gushing
of my arteries' blood.
All sensations fall away
into quietude.

With the last trace of breath gone,
My body vanishes.

Floating in immense emptiness,
submerging in cosmic silence,
without any sense of self,
losing all my boundaries,
on the edge of the horizon,
I disappear into a
     vast     awareness.

Coming back,
the quiet echoes
through my empty body.

I have traversed the void,
the fullest emptiness
I have ever glimpsed,
shimmering with infinite
creative potentials.

My heart explodes.
No longer am I a tiny speck,
the universe is in me.

Stock photo selected to
illustrate the poem, "Meditation"

# GRATITUDE

# Gratitude

Sam Yau

Step inside your favorite café,
look into the eyes of a waitress
who has served you for years,
ask, "How are you?" with
a thankful smile.
Notice what arises inside you.

Feel the cup of latte
warm your hands.
Let its delicate, sweet flavor
mellow your heart.

Behind the barista,
can you see
the farmers, the processors, the distributors
from the four corners of the world
toiling to create this delight to start your day?

How the window is eager to show you
the golden sunset over the Pacific,
the stair tread to rise to receive
your next step as you ascend,
the kettle to whistle
a love song,
the oven to ooze the
delicious aroma of baking croissants?

How the patient rocks grinded
against the ocean waves for eons
to turn into the finest white sands
to cuddle your feet on the beach?

How floating moisture, dust, and wind
create the most gorgeous shape-
shifting clouds to dazzle you?

How the sun and the moon take turns
to illuminate you from the sky?

Can you see,
every encounter
is an exchange of love?

How everything around you is alive,
forever saying, "I love you"?

Gratitude unlocks
the hidden intimacy you
already have with everything.

# COME HOME

# Come Home

*Sam Yau*

You were a primal bundle of joy.
You were the scream, the tears, the smile.
You felt everything in your body,
and let it pass through you.

As you grew up, life sometimes
presented you with a little more
agony and anguish than you could bear.

You learned to run away from it,
you would bury yourself in a book,
distract yourself from your pain
by thinking.
You would conceptualize,
escape into analysis,
relish the elation of synthesis,
be pleased with your rationalization.

You adored theories built
upon layers of abstraction.
You would see a tree, and
rather than running your hand along
the lines and wrinkles on the trunk,
or sniffing sticky fragrant sap, or tracing
the veins flowing through the leaves,
your mind would categorize it.

You were a walking brain
dragging your body behind you.

Unexpressed feelings knotted your muscles,
wrapped you up like a mummy.

Let yourself feel again.
Set yourself free.
Come home to your body.

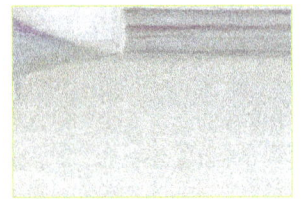

# DEVOUR

# Devour

Sam Yau

Before morning peeks around the curtain's edge,
before the memory of last night's dreams starts to fade,
before I am hijacked by mental chatter,
in the twilight between asleep and awake,

I lie still.
Find my breath.
Sense my rhythm.
Tune in to what I'm feeling
in my body,
without thinking,
without judging.

If the feeling has a color, I
let it seep across my entire field of vision,
soak every cell of mine in its hue.

Sometimes it is a golden lifting-up.
Other times, it is a gray heaviness in my chest,
if I stay long enough with it,
I reach its opposite.

If the feeling has a taste, I
swish it around in my mouth,
savor it with my electrified taste buds.
Some mornings are easier than others.
But I don't try to cover it.

I leave no trace of my hangover—
I devour it,
lick my palate clean,
start fresh for a new day.

Original painting by Olena Zavakevych
inspired by the poem, "Devour"

# A THOUSAND small cuts

A Thousand Small Cuts
Grief
Darkness
Split
Tapestry

# A THOUSAND SMALL CUTS

# A Thousand Small Cuts

**Sam Yau**

You can't recall a single
major traumatic event.

But you have suffered
small but recurrent hurts
inflicted by those closest to you
over many years:

You'd walk in a room
and feel invisible,
your enthusiasm was negated,
your idea, brushed off
and called clueless.

No one to talk to.
No one cares.

Trapped.

Small unhealed injuries
snowball into a
debilitating wound.

It gnaws at your self-worth,
depletes your life-force.
The world feels unsafe,
you become a loner.

Your pain body unlivable,
bit by bit, your soul leaves.
Your eyes look vacant.
Nothing is pleasurable.

A chunk of your life has
vanished from memory.

A thousand cuts need
a thousand doses
of loving kindness
to heal.

Open your heart,
be vulnerable,
share your life with
friends old and new.

Look for beauty, love's
favorite place to indwell.

Your favorite things
will come to life and return
your caring vibes.

Propagate your love,
for it boomerangs,
multiplies,
and heals you at the root.

Original painting by Olena Zavakevych
inspired by the poem, "A Thousand Small Cuts"

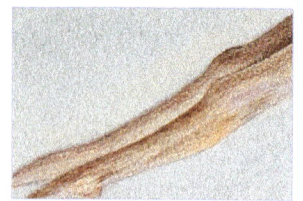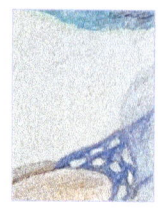

# GRIEF

# Grief

Sam Yau

Let it cocoon you,
dissolve you
into an amorphous,
excruciating brew,

form imaginal discs
from which
you will emerge.

Spill your tears,
or it will immobilize you.

Let it speak,
or it will silence you.

Do not shun
front-row seats:

suffering
death
mortality.

Grief expands you.

Let grief embrace you,
let it unfurl
love and anger,
guilt and peace,
all at once.

Eclose—love's permanence
shines through
grief's exit.

Original painting by Olena Zavakevych
inspired by the poem, "Grief"

# DARKNESS

# Darkness

**Sam Yau**

Despair lingers
in the night,
it is a darkness
with no exit.

I can't overcome
my lead-heavy chest
to get out of bed.
I draw the curtains tight
against the dark clouds closing in.

I wake up to the late afternoon sun.
I drag myself to the trail
on the ridge facing the Pacific.

Last night's rain—
transmuted into gorgeous clouds
aflame in gold and red in the sunset.

The long shadows
of the town below.

I wait for the moon to rise,
reflected in the ocean,
whispering in the ebb and flow
of the tide.

The moon descends below the hills,
stars glitter in the black velvet sky,
lightning illuminates distant dark clouds.

The moon will wax
and wane.
The seasons will cycle.
Rest in the unknowing.
Sleep soundly tonight.

**Photo by Sam Yau
for the poem, "Darkness"**

# SPLIT

# Split
### Sam Yau

You are a mansion with many rooms.
Some with doors that open,
some that are locked forever.
Some barricaded by blocked memories
you don't even know exist.

The knocking
at the door of your
conscious awareness
never stops.

In the furthest recesses
lives a three-year-old in perpetual rage,
ready to avenge
the unimaginable abuse
she has suffered.

Down the hall is the young girl
who plays mother,
tries to soothe,
hold back the
violent tantrums.

There is the fairy princess
living in her tower,
completely shielded.

The tough adolescent boy
hangs out in the garage,
avoiding further abuse
by becoming the abuser internalized,
the bully turned inward,
policing the gang inside.

The young woman
who meditates to remain calm
amid chaos and pain.

The intellectual
who talks philosophy
and lives in his head,
making sure no one pops up
at the wrong time,
in the wrong place.

*Continued*

Each bore witness to a wounding.
Each with their own
unique divine spark.

They appear and vanish,
you attempt to calm them,
to numb your pain
with vodka,
you are in chaos
and exhaustion.

The journey
of healing
is arduous.

Each personality
is here for you
to love,
to transform, and
to integrate.

You are brave.
You are whole,
shining in the
harmony and brilliance
of unity in your multiplicity.

# TAPESTRY

# Tapestry

**Sam Yau**

An angel appears.
I ask her to expand
my empathy.

An eye's blink,
I am engulfed in
swirling images:

The Inquisition.
The World Wars.
Auschwitz.
The Nanking Massacre.

A hammer slams
into my heart.
Heat melts me
from within.

I wake up soaked in sweat.
My heart pounds.

I need an antidote.
How do I hold such agony?
I ask the angel to return me to sleep.

Afloat in a dreamy field
of iridescent orange and purple poppies,
in a panorama of
splendor and radiance,
I am infused with
beauty and love.

Horrific images
return and interweave,
exacerbated by

wailing,
shrieking,
cursing—

reaching the sky.

All of a sudden,

my perception
conflates into a
harmonious tapestry,
rustling on the waves
of a symphonic melody.

Original painting by Olena Zavakevych
inspired by the poem, "Tapestry"

# TRANSFIGURED

Transfigured
Walk With Me, My Son
Unblemished
My Spirit Friends

# TRANSFIGURED

# Transfigured

*Sam Yau*

When you put a bullet
through your brain,
you were only 27.

You used to tell me how
you'd sit alone in the park,
watching others in silence.

Dissociated, you said
you felt like a ghost,
an alien who didn't belong.

One scene after another,
you'd relive each trauma
like a vivid full-sensory
replay, in endless loops
you couldn't escape.

You withdrew from life to
avoid all possible triggers,
stayed in your dimly lit room
with the curtains drawn,
a prisoner of your fear.

You'd wake up wishing
you were still asleep,
you'd sleep, wishing
you'd never wake up,

in between,
you'd drink whisky
to numb your pain
until you puked.

With tears streaming
down your face,
you told me it was too late,
your brain had been damaged—
the alarm kept blasting
even when there was no fire—
it would not stop enflaming
past traumas in your mind.

You were a runaway car with
no brakes on your anger and
the gas pedal stuck to the floor.

I would hug you
and tell you
you would live.

You told me
you were already dead.

*Continued*

# Transfigured

**Sam Yau**

My heart was shattered
in a million pieces.
Fear gripped me,
my pulse pounded,
my body shook.

When I heard that
you were gone,
there was an explosion
of love for you in my heart.

I feel closer to you every day.

I see you everywhere—
a baby in a carrier,
a boy running to his dad,
a young man in a café,
birds, clouds…

It is my turn to be
endlessly triggered.

I never knew about the
bottomless well
of tears in me.

Your light has never dimmed.

You are so loved.
Your soul never carries
a trace of injury.

You have forgiven all who
hurt you in human life.

You time-travel back to
feel the love of
family and friends
you couldn't perceive then.

You have signed up
to help mortals suffering
in the same way
from the other side.

I have been
dreaming of
my next life,
of being with you again,
to do a better job of
loving and
protecting you.

Will you let me be
your dad again?

Original painting by Olena Zavakevych
inspired by the poem, "Transfigured"

# WALK WITH ME, MY SON

## Walk with Me, My Son

#### Sam Yau

I can't remember how many times my heart was pierced
as you shared your inner torments all those lonely years.

Avoiding triggers from past traumas, you cage
and lock yourself in a curtain-drawn room in despair.
The wounded child in you turns into a monster in rage.
Intrusions of painful flashbacks are looping on a tear.

There're days of warm sunrays breaking through black clouds.
Oh, your soul in the dark night, maybe you can make it through.
Able to feel and receive love, your hope starts to sprout.
As better days turn sparse, you fall back into your groove.

A few times, you emerge from sinking to gasp for air.
Tired of fights between your inner Jekyll and Hyde,
to finish Hyde, you also end the endless pain you fear.
With no human body, you know the real you are neither.

My computer chimes all night—messages with no words.
An uninvited melody plays itself—a siren song of death.
The call from your disconnected number—greeted by silence.
I can't miss your presence, you give me so many signs.
Salient clouds dance in the sky: you're well in your soul.

You crack my heart wide open to feel the deep suffering of the world.
I tumble down the tunnel of grief to find some peace on the other side.
You inspire me to live in my soul and sense the beauty of your realm.
Walk with me, till the day I reach the distant clouds where you reside.

Photo by Sam Yau for the poem,
"Walk with Me, My Son"

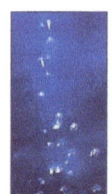

# UNBLEMISHED

# Unblemished

**Sam Yau**

Do not cry when
I return to spirit.
Rejoice.

My heart was broken,
but I am not shattered.

My mind was fractured,
but I am whole.

My body was wrecked,
but my soul is unblemished.

Trauma never tarnished
the light emanating from me.

I was perfect in
my imperfections.

The toils of living—
sagging skin,
wrinkled face,
sloth-like movement—
left no trace on
my etheric body.

Forever young
and ravishing,
I will traverse realms
in a flash.

I will see
in all directions,
be anywhere in an instant
with mere intention.

I will soar into the light,
a garden exploding
with roses and harps,
surrounded by
peaceful mountains,
embraced by
all my loved ones
on the other side.

I see divinity
in all of creation:
love is its essence.

Original painting by Olena Zavakevych
inspired by the poem, "Unblemished"

# MY SPIRIT FRIENDS

## My Spirit Friends

Sam Yau

I know you well—
not by your names,
but by your energies.

Tragedy has cracked
my heart wide open.

I can't bear witness
to so much suffering
in this world.

I can't return to my
former insulated self.

It is heavy here.
I want to float away.
It is confining here.
I long to be free.
I can't breathe here.
I pray to go home.

But I must stay.
There are still tasks
I must complete.

Spirit friends,
gather close,
I am still,
merge with me,
let us join hands,
fuse minds,
sync our hearts.

I pray my vision
opens to your seeing,
my mind to your knowing,
my heart to your compassion.

Inspire me,
lift me up,
fill me with joy,
grant me peace.

Above all,
expand and bolster
this vessel of mine
to be a conduit of
your love and wisdom
for the world.

Help me to
straddle both worlds,
but ground me in this reality.

# SCIENCE AND *consciousness*

Science and Consciousness
The Gravity of Love
Collide
My Body

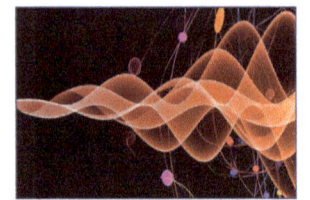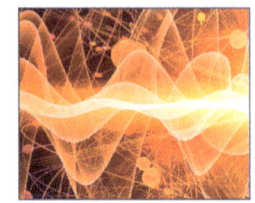

# SCIENCE AND CONSCIOUSNESS

# Science and Consciousness

# Sam Yau

Copernicus dislodged earth from the center of the cosmos.
Newton discovered the laws of movements of heavenly stars.
Darwin dethroned humans to a humbler origin in evolution.
Einstein's imagination uncovered secret spacetime's creation.

With towering discoveries, science proclaims matter over mind.
Laws of nature in the macroscopic world have been settled.
All things nonphysical, idealistic, spiritual have dwindled.

Consciousness is a mere epiphenomenon of the brain.
Myths, philosophy, and poetry are fine to pursue, if only
you know they are peripheral to the neurons in the cortex.
Unverifiable subjective experiences are of little interest.

Alas, with this view, the cosmos is dispirited and disenchanted.
The profundity of human's inner experiences is diminished.

Then comes Quantum Mechanics of the microscopic world.

This tiniest speck of matter exists as a probability equation,
refuses to manifest itself unless probed by a human observer,
defies the speed-of-light limit of Einstein's $E=mc^2$ calculation,
appears and disappears into thin air like a little magical fairy.
Once connected, a pair of subatomic particles spin,
across a vast cosmic distance, in perfect coordination.

*Continued*

Independence of observed from observer is no longer preserved.
The myth of a deterministic and objective universe is shattered.
With the mighty edifice of Newtonian Physics now toppled,
the nature of matter before observation remains a riddle.

I hear Quantum Mechanics whisper in my ear:

*Even the tiny quark is imbued with consciousness.*
*For every outer matter, there is an inner awareness.*

*This is the realm of subjective experience*
*beyond the grasp of science:*

*where feelings, intuition,*
*imagination and meaning reign,*
*where poetry is composed,*
*philosophy is ideated,*
*scientific hypotheses are inspired,*

*where our soul speaks to us,*
*and Divinity reveals its Face.*

Stock photo selected to illustrate
the poem, "Science and Consciousness"

# THE GRAVITY OF LOVE

# The Gravity of Love

*Sam Yau*

Who choreographs the oscillations
of tiny strings of energy?
Who sets the frequencies
of the dazzling varieties of elements?

We are quarks and electrons
which are 99.99% empty.
Who projects solidity from emptiness
to stage the illusion of physicality?

Quarks in our nuclei zigzag
near the speed of light.
Who creates this mirage of stillness?

A subatomic particle emerges
from its hidden superposition only
when we consciously look for it.
Who instill it with the intelligence
to play hide-and-seek with us?

Once connected, two particles behave
as one—even when they are
across the cosmos from each other.
Who imbues this immutable entanglement?

We are dancing lights effusing from mysterious
and interpenetrating clouds of probabilities.

We involute from divine to human,
dosed with forgetfulness and narrowed perception,
to evolve and find our way back to source.

We live in multiple dimensions.
Higher planes spill over—
clairvoyance,
precognition,
synchronicity.
Imagination is
knowledge from the future.

We project our inner world onto
our outer reality, unaware that
we are holograms of our souls.

Gravity holds us in spacetime,
stitched together by entanglement.
In its deepest core is love,
the finest substance
and most powerful force
in the universe.

Stock photo selected to
illustrate the poem, "The Gravity of Love"

# COLLIDE

HIGGS BOSON - GOD'S PARTICLE CONFIRMED

# Collide

## Sam Yau

A curiosity worth more than
thirteen billion dollars,
wider than a seventeen-mile oval tunnel,
deeper than five hundred feet below the ground,
bigger than any one country's agenda.

In a trillionth of a second,
a man-made collision opens
a portal to another dimension,
a new Big Bang after fourteen billion years.

Protons one hundred thousand times
hotter than the sun collide
at the speed of light.

Trillions of known
and yet-to-be-discovered
sparkling filaments
emerge and explode.

Amid the thundering, deafening maelstrom,
hear the whisper of a Higgs boson,
the wizard behind the curtain
bestowing mass on
ghostly subatomic specks.

The invisible massless is transformed
into the visible physical,
appears from nothing,
disappears into nothing,
shapeshifts from waves to matter
and back again.

Entangled in an unbroken web
of the holographic universe,
there are no lonely quarks.

Imagine a human world with
no illusion of separation.

Stock photo selected to
illustrate the poem, "Collide"

# MY BODY

# My Body

## Sam Yau

Suck all the empty space out of me,
   like letting all the air out of a balloon.
   My quarks and electrons whirl and tumble.

   I collapse into a grain of sand,
   blown far with a whip of breeze.

   I ask where I am,
   but find me     nowhere.

   And who is asking?

# SEE WITH *the eyes of our heart*

See with the Eyes of Our Heart
I Can't Wait to Meet You
Infused
Wine Tasting
Shadow
Reverberate
Parting

  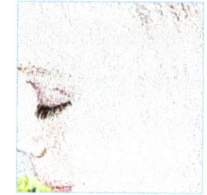 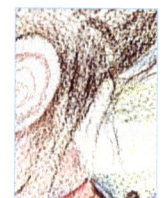  

# SEE WITH THE EYES OF OUR HEART

# See with the Eyes of Our Heart

*Sam Yau*

An angel visits me in a dream, says,
*Come. I will show you faces:*

A homeless veteran is curled up on a street corner.
He relives his battle; comrades fall around him.
Flashbacks come one after the other like beads on a string.
He morphs into my son, who suffered
from PTSD for years and took his life at 27.
My eyes swell with teary love for him.

The girl I was infatuated with when I was a shy
fifteen-year-old wanders down the aisle of a grocery store.
I never had the courage to tell her how I felt.
Tenderness ripples across the pond of my heart,
fresh as the first time I laid eyes upon her.

A child chases swirling clouds along a hill's ridge.
Her face lights up at the sight of a heart-shaped rock.
Brilliant red camellias fill her with wonder.
Pine trees aglow with fondness twinkle
at her, gleam in her eyes.

# See with the Eyes of Our Heart

Sam Yau

A volunteer dries and clothes the shivering body of a
fragile blind, mute, and deaf old man with tender care
at Mother Teresa's mission in Calcutta.
He guides the stranger-brother to the dining room and the
elder's face is transfigured into the luminous face of Jesus.

A mother folds her baby's clothes in the laundry room.
She holds the soft terry against her face and
imagines looking into the eyes of her baby in her arms.

Love remembers, waits behind every eye on every face,
within every flower and every tree.

Our deepest losses crack our hearts open,
a heart connection impregnates life with meaning,
our world is held within the gaze between mother and child,
the mundane is unmasked as sacred,
divinity is all around.

Original painting by Olena Zavakevych
inspired by the poem, "See with the Eyes of Our Heart"

# I CAN'T WAIT TO MEET YOU

When I see your face for the first time,
you lift your gaze to meet mine.
Time freezes.
Everyone else fades away.
We know our destiny.

Fired-up neurons trance-dance in unison.
We dive into each other with no fear.

We soar to heaven, sink to hell,
unleash our best and our worst,
mirror each other's light and shadow.
We grind at each other's humanness.
In joy, in pain, we grow together.

No matter how many times
we separate and reunite,
we always find our way back
to one another.

We recognize our original faces,
remember our eternal bond,
intertwined for many lifetimes,
forever in each other's embrace.

To see and be seen
in our soul-essence
is to be in God's presence.

Original painting by Olena Zavakevych
inspired by the poem, "I Can't Wait to Meet You"

# INFUSED

A circle of lime trees
outstretch their branches for us
to lie beneath their canopy.
The leaves rustle in the gentle breeze,
shimmer in the morning sun.

Above the foliage, clouds swirl-waltz
against the satiny blue sky, celebrating
the melding of two kindred spirits.

Song thrushes fly-dance above us, chirping:
*There is a place for us, us alone.*

You lay your hand on mine
while we lie on the green grass.
A fireball stoked by our hearts
twirls between our palms.
We are floating up, up and away.

The fire you ignited in my soul
is burning bright,
spreading out of control.

I am infused with you.
I am drunk in our co-vibrations.

Your hand has never left.
Maybe it never will.

# WINE TASTING

# Wine Tasting

## Sam Yau

I've been the person
who'd fall for
the first one
who came along.

This time,
I'd change.

I would

look,
swirl,
sniff,
sip
and savor

the exquisitely curated
rich varietals
in the perfect
sequence.

But I can no longer
delude myself;

can't hide behind
an idyllic new life
you're not the
      center of—

my fear of
being trapped
in a single taste.

This morning,
I woke up engulfed
in the pain of the
looming separation.

How I would
pine for you
when the iron bird
fades into the cloud,

How I would
run away
in clever ways,
only to find
your face swirling
in my heart.

Once more,
I tore the
tasting menu
to pieces.

There is only one.

Stock photo selected to
illustrate the poem, "Wine Tasting"

# SHADOW

# Shadow

*Sam Yau*

The day I met you, I burst through my heart
and rocketed to the edge of the universe and back.

I know of no love so boundless, so freeing.
It demands nothing of you, it rejects nothing in you.

Day after day, your soul's blinding light shines through.
Facet by facet, your iridescent radiance grows until

you become the sun, the moon, and all the stars in the sky.
You catapult me right into the center of my divinity.

I stand naked in front of you, immersed in your luminosity, unaware
that the shadow flicker-dances with the shimmering like friends.

The foreboding of the inevitable breakup looms. The distant heartache,
beat by beat, leaches out the bubbling joy from the now.

When you show me your blazing love poem to your previous lover,
a vinegar-fed fire snakes its green scorching flame from my stomach to my heart.

Light and shadow, love and jealousy, are not strange bedfellows.
It is me who is inflicted. Your pristineness remains unblemished.

I wish I could be in the moment, lost in the bliss of my love for you.
I wish I could scatter the future, or my fear of it, in the capricious wind.

    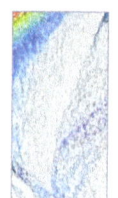 

# REVERBERATE

# Reverberate

**Sam Yau**

See the gem
through the grime.

Discover each poem—
a facet of my soul.

Witness the sparkle,
reflect it back to me,
let me face my radiance.

I am awed by
your luminosity.
I mirror it back to you.

We embrace
each other's shadow.

We won't be lonely again.

Time and distance freeze,
conversations and feelings
pick up where they left off.

Geography may keep us apart,
but when we are together,
it is like coming home.

As light and mirror,
we illuminate,
reflect,
inspire
each other
without end.

Where lights reverberate,
the soul sings with joy.

Original painting by Olena Zavakevych
inspired by the poem, "Reverberate"

# PARTING

# Parting

### Sam Yau

Our broken togetherness,
   built over nineteen years,
   still has a will to survive.

It doesn't accept its demise with grace.
It wriggles and flips in the air,
a fish out of water
gasping its dying breath.

Nothing to talk about
other than our child.

We were in the same house,
but seldom in the same room.
We'd try to connect—one of us
always threw up our hands.

I don't want us
to repaint the past in grey,
to smear the sunny side
of our partnership.

I want us to honor the light
and shadow in each of us,
tread our blame lightly,
lest we banish years
behind the door of oblivion.

The dawn is just below the horizon.
I wait in silence in the thinning darkness.
When the first ray of light peers through
the fog,
a new day will begin for both of us.

We don't have to figure everything out,
relationships are complex;
a combination of karma and freewill
and mystery, too.

# NATURE

Nature

The Effortless Way of Tao

Swept Away by the
   Tiniest Vibrations

Clouds

# NATURE

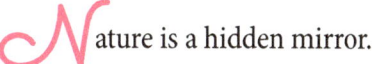ature is a hidden mirror.

If you love nature,
it will love you back
manyfold.

If you seek the truth,
Nature will reveal to you
the secrets of the Universe.

If you seek beauty,
Nature will dazzle you with
its breathtaking grandeur
invisible to the heedless.

Nature is alive.
It is impartial.
It mirrors and responds
to your inner world,
only if you are aware.

**Stock photo selected to
illustrate the poem, "Nature"**

# THE EFFORTLESS WAY OF TAO

# The Effortless Way of Tao

## Sam Yau

The river of Tao flows into eternity.
Embraces all things.
Nourishes all lives.
Permeates all high and low spaces.
Deep or shallow, calm or turbulent,
its meandering is effortless.

The clouds of Tao have shapeshifted for eons.
Against the blue-sky canvas, they morph—
a towering cathedral, a fire-breathing dragon,
a giant flying Pterosaurs, a swirling UFO.
They arrive unannounced and depart without a trace.
Their whimsical creative explosion is effortless.

The sage of Tao stays in inner silence:
plain, simple, humble.
She is innately kind.
She speaks volumes with few words,
accomplishes much without striving.
Her strength comes from her softness,
her compassion from her unity with all.
Accepting the ebb and flow of life,
content with inner peace,
seeking no external glory,
her life is effortless.

Tao cannot be named or spoken.
It precedes Heaven and Earth.
It is the Mother of all things,
the Formless that manifests all forms,
the Void that outpours like an inexhaustible well,
the Stillness that springs into spontaneous right actions.
It can be glimpsed by observing Nature.

Tao is our true nature to be cultivated.
At one with Tao, our life becomes effortless,
like the river and the clouds.

Stock photo selected for
the poem, "The Effortless Way of Tao"

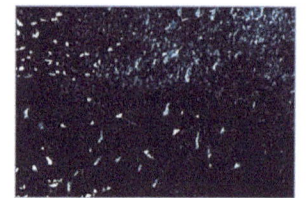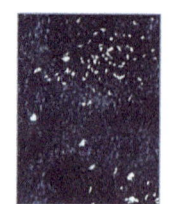

# SWEPT AWAY BY THE TINIEST VIBRATIONS

# Swept Away by the Tiniest Vibrations

*Sam Yau*

I stand against the whipping wind.
I don't want to leave.
I stretch my hands out to catch my balance.
Tremors rumble up from the center of the planet.

Tidal waves made of the
tiniest vibrations wash over me.
My billion cells trance-dance in unison.

Minuscule filaments of energy
deep within me oscillate and throb
like little golden champagne bubbles of joy,
ready to explode and celebrate.

The dancing ocean glitters with silver,
reflecting the moon above.

The space occupied by my body
is now only vibration.
This is the essence of my organs, my metabolism,
my breath, my movements, my existence.
I am rhythm expanding outward.

The whole universe consists of this
majestic, jubilant, life-giving pulsation.

My body sways with the wind.
My feet are planted deep into the earth.
I am an ancient sequoia.
I am in my element.
I am home.
I want to stay here
for eternity.

Original painting by Olena Zavakevych
inspired by the poem, "Swept Away by the Tiniest Vibrations"

# CLOUDS

# Clouds

**Sam Yau**

I love to gaze skyward
and greet my friends.

Gold sunbeams pour
like three layers of a
cascading waterfall
into the Pacific.

A dome
floats around me:
stratocumuli
like massive cotton balls
form the bottom,
and streaks
of white wisps
reach up to create the
celestial ceiling.

Successive layers form
a cloud staircase that reaches
from the ground up to
the only patch of blue in the sky.

A black hawk rises like a spirit
through the menacing, swirling,
dark thunderheads
toward the cloud-cloaked sun.

At sunset, cumulus form
a giant upturned hand,
holding the setting orb.
Luminous rays spray
through the space
between its fingers
into the twilight ocean.

The homeward sun's reflection
forms a fiery candle in the ocean
against the crimson red sky.

Clouds dance
without attachment
across the azure sky.
They collide into each other
with utmost gentleness.

After rain,
transmutation.
The sky will be gorgeous
tomorrow morning.

Photo by Sam Yau
for the poem, "Clouds"

**Second photo by Sam Yau
for the poem, "Clouds"**

**Third photo by Sam Yau
for the poem, "Clouds"**

# DUENDE

Duende
Kathmandu 2003
Ode to Lucille Clifton

# DUENDE

# Duende

Sam Yau

You don't know me,
but I've known you for eons.
I follow you, life after life,
to awaken the artist in you.

I am the part of you
that is moonstruck by romance,
awed by the sunset's glory,
beguiled by the beauty of a poem,
entranced by African drumming.

I was never born.
I will never die.

Until the day
you stare down death's eyes,
become fearless,
you can't know me
and live your art.

It is I who
    swirls in dervishes,
    stomps in flamenco,
    improvises in jazz.

I am the primal sensual,
your carnal pleasure.
I am the titillating passionate,
your happiness.

Intellect relinquishes its grip
when I step onstage,
your body under my spell,

    you and your art become one.

Awestruck and breathless,
    time pauses,
    all else vanishes.
What remains—

    the eternal moment of joy

you long to return to
again and again.

I am your Duende,
    your soul.

Original painting by Olena Zavakevych
inspired by the poem, "Duende"

# KATHMANDU 2003

# Kathmandu 2003

Sam Yau

Summer heat soaks the air, rickshaws and
cars meander along the dust-clouded streets

drivers cuss, beep and blast their horn
cows, unmoved, block traffic, lay more dung

stray dogs bark amidst toxic haze
riders spew sputum from clogged lungs

brilliant colors of spices on a wheeled cart dart my eyes
exotic birds for sale in wired cages flutter their wings in vain

a monkey perched on an overhanging tree branch swoops down
to snatch a half-eaten apple from my astounded palm

an old yogi with roped hair and a toothless smile stands on one leg
charmers on stone steps play flute to lure slithering snakes to dance

a young mother-beggar clasps her deformed child with big sad eyes
pungent sewage and sweet incense pierce and startle my breath

the embalmed in flamboyant clothes burnt in open air
between wood piles on the banks of the Ganges

ashes scatter in the river where children play
vultures feast on floating singed remains

# Kathmandu 2003

*Sam Yau*

as the pyre releases the smoke of death
the eternal soul is liberated, heaven-bound

devotees bow under giant eyes painted on temple walls
Shiva, Shakti, Ganesh seem to materialize all around

blue, white, red, green and yellow prayer flags flap
rows of golden prayer wheels swirl

surrounded by towering ice-capped mountains
the plethora of color, sound and smell overwhelm my senses

I float between the silent snow and Kathmandu's bustling ground
a tapestry of heaven and earth, mundane and sacred, in perfect harmony

Stock photo selected to illustrate
the poem, "Kathmandu 2003"

# ODE TO LUCILLE CLIFTON

## Ode to Lucille Clifton

Sam Yau

On the day of your passing,
you lift the veil of transition,
walk through a five-pace fog

a wild river flows above,
shimmering the blood-red
of the moon's edge

Jesus would not miss it, neither
would Yemoja or Kali

millions flock to the gates of heaven
to thank you for the virtue and dignity
they gleaned from your words while
living their humble lives on earth

your poems—    short, unadorned,
punctuated with silence, sparseness,
their essence sculpted on a kitchen table
surrounded by six children, living and dead—
imbue the mundane with the sacred

you did not shy away from life's horrors,
truth-telling in the plainest ways,
but always with optimism and love:
that gist of your soul that gushes from
every pore of your body that you adore

you are the bridge people cross to
find the real strength in their spirit

you rise again
and rise again
to dance

# A SUMMONS to lightworkers

A Summons to Lightworkers

   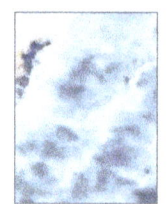  

# A SUMMONS TO LIGHTWORKERS

On this blueish planet of ours,
a tiny twinkle among billions
of brilliant swirling galaxies,
lies a grand cosmic journey,
an evolution of consciousness,
an ascension from matter to spirit.

Humanity has veered off-course
   from Prehistory,
   through the Dark Ages,
   to the Renaissance
   to the Industrial/Scientific/Information Age,
and is still searching for
   the Promised Land.

We are obsessed with
   gratifying the senses and intellect
instead of
   awaking to our true identity,
   our soul,

the essence of which,
   is love.

This divine spark
buried deep inside each of us,
its radiance untarnished,
still awaits to be lived.

# A Summons to Lightworkers

*Sam Yau*

People crowd into
   the temple of technology,
bow to
   the golden calf of data,
salivate for
   the spoils of artificial intelligence,
all under the auspices of
   scientific materialism.

Idealizing comfort,
   not peace or joy.

True power lies in the heart,
compassion for all sentient beings,
the awakening to divinity within
and its union with humanity.

Love stitches the fabric of gravity
in the curvature of spacetime
the universe cradles.

The strongest force
is hidden in
   the smallest nucleus,
   the softest heart,
   the plainest love.

We, the lightworkers
blessed and humbled by
a taste of the union with the Divine,
must rev up earth's vibrations,
wake humanity to its destiny of
heaven on earth.

Photo by Sam for the poem,
"A Summons to Lightworkers"

# ABOUT THE POET

**Sam Yau** is a retired business executive, splitting his time between managing his investments and writing poetry.

Sam has re-invented his life several times, from a 6-month baby on a refugee boat, to a penniless student from a distant land, to the CEO of a billion-dollar corporation, to the Chairman of a well-known pioneering center for personal growth, to a poet who writes about soul's journey, life's vicissitudes, trauma and healing, consciousness, science and spirituality, and mysticism.

Sam has an MBA in Finance with University of Chicago. Sam is a single parent living with his 14-year daughter in Laguna Beach. Sam enjoys music, hiking, and active travel around the world.

Sam can be reached at sam@samyaupoetry.com.

# ABOUT THE ARTIST

**Olena Zavakevych**, seeker of spiritual truths, and former TV journalist and anchor, met Sam at the Omega Institute in Rhinebeck, New York. She was enchanted by Sam's honesty and fearless expression of his personal journey through poetry.

Olena got her first degree in economics. Then, while on the other side of the monumental Iron Curtain, she witnessed its crumbling first-hand. She become eager to explore the world and soon lived in many countries. Later, the bright and multicultural Houston became her home.

Olena has worked as an art teacher, muralist, gallery manager, film consultant, and restoration artist. She graduated from the prestigious Glassell School of Art, MFAH. Illustrating poetry is her present and most gratifying endeavor. She is passionate about and dedicated to the expansion of human consciousness.

www.ingramcontent.com/pod-product-compliance
Lightning Source LLC
Chambersburg PA
CBHW051119110526
44589CB00026B/2978